Executive Summary

The long wars in Iraq and Afghanistan have cost the United States in many ways. For the American Armed Forces, the human toll has been profound: as of November 9, 2007, 4,578 American soldiers have lost their lives, and 30,205 have been wounded, many of them gravely. The damage to our international reputation at a time when the United States faces grave security challenges all over the world has also been severe. And the full economic costs of the war to the American taxpayers and the overall U.S. economy go well beyond even the immense federal budget costs already reported. These "hidden costs" of the Iraq war include the ongoing drain on U.S. economic growth created by Iraq-related borrowing, the disruptive effects of the conflict on world oil markets, the future care of our injured veterans, repair costs for the military, and other undisclosed costs.

In this report, the Joint Economic Committee estimates the total costs of the long war in Iraq to the American economy as a whole:

- The total economic costs of the wars in Iraq and Afghanistan so far have been approximately double the total amounts directly requested by the Administration to fight these wars.

- The future economic costs of a prolonged military presence in Iraq would be massive. Even assuming a considerable drawdown in troop levels, total economic costs of the wars in Iraq and Afghanistan (with the vast majority of costs a result of in the war Iraq) would amount to $3.5 trillion between 2003 and 2017. This is over $1 trillion higher than the recent Congressional Budget Office (CBO) Federal cost forecast for the same scenario, which counted only direct spending and interest paid on war-related debt resulting from that spending.

- The total economic cost of the war in Iraq to a family of four is a shocking $16,500 from 2002 to 2008. When the war in Afghanistan is included, the burden to the American family rises to $20,900. The future impact on a family of four skyrockets to $36,900 for Iraq and $46,400 for Iraq and Afghanistan when all potential costs from 2002 to 2017 are included.

The American people and Democrats in Congress have urged a dramatic change of course in Iraq. This war has cost Americans far too much, in terms of lives, dollars, and our reputation around the world. This report also demonstrates that a change in course would bring substantial economic savings to our country.

Through 2008, the True Cost of the War has been Double the Administration's Budgeted Cost

To date, the President has requested a total of $607 billion for the Iraq war alone since 2003. This is over ten times higher than the $50 to $60 billion cost estimated by the Administration prior to the start of the war. Costs have increased every year since the start of the war in 2003. The Administration has requested $804 billion for the Iraq and Afghanistan wars combined (CRS 2007, Bumiller 2003).[1]

To provide some perspective on these figures, just the funds requested for the Iraq war through 2008 would have been sufficient to provide health insurance coverage to all of America's uninsured for the 2003-2008 period. (There were approximately 45 million uninsured Americans at the start of the war in 2003 and this number rose to 47 million by 2006, which is the latest figure available from the U.S. Census Bureau).

But even beyond these direct fiscal impacts, there are a large number of costs that do not appear directly in Administration funding requests for the Iraq war. The most important of these include the following:

- **Borrowed money to finance the Iraq War has displaced productive investment.** Since taxes have been cut and other spending has increased since the beginning of the Iraq war, it seems clear that the war has been and continues to be funded using borrowed money. The increase in government borrowing displaces substantial amounts of productive investment by U.S. businesses, thus reducing productivity in the economy over many future years. Interest costs paid by taxpayers are only a subset of these costs.

- **Substantial Iraq-related costs have been borrowed from foreigners**. The interest payments on this debt constitute a flow of funds from Americans to those foreigners who have bought our debt.

Table 1: Requested Appropriations and Total Costs Accrued So Far Period: FY 2002-2008		
	IRAQ WAR ONLY	**IRAQ AND AFGHANISTAN**
Direct Appropriations*	$607 Billion	$804 Billion
Total Costs**	$1.3 Trillion	$1.6 Trillion
Costs per Family of Four***	$16,500	$20,900

Budget costs in nominal dollars, flow of economic costs discounted to the relevant budget year. See Appendix B for discussion of methodology.
* Based on CRS and CBO cost estimates of direct appropriations. Includes Administration's FY 2008 request for war funding, which has not been passed by Congress.
** Based on total sum of present value costs accrued in each budgetary year from 2002-2008
*** Total over 2002-2008 period.

---

[1] As of November 2007, the Congress had already appropriated $449 billion of spending on Iraq, and $609 billion for both Iraq and Afghanistan combined.

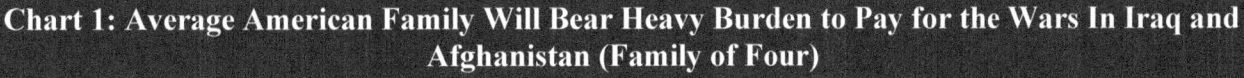

Chart 1: Average American Family Will Bear Heavy Burden to Pay for the Wars In Iraq and Afghanistan (Family of Four)

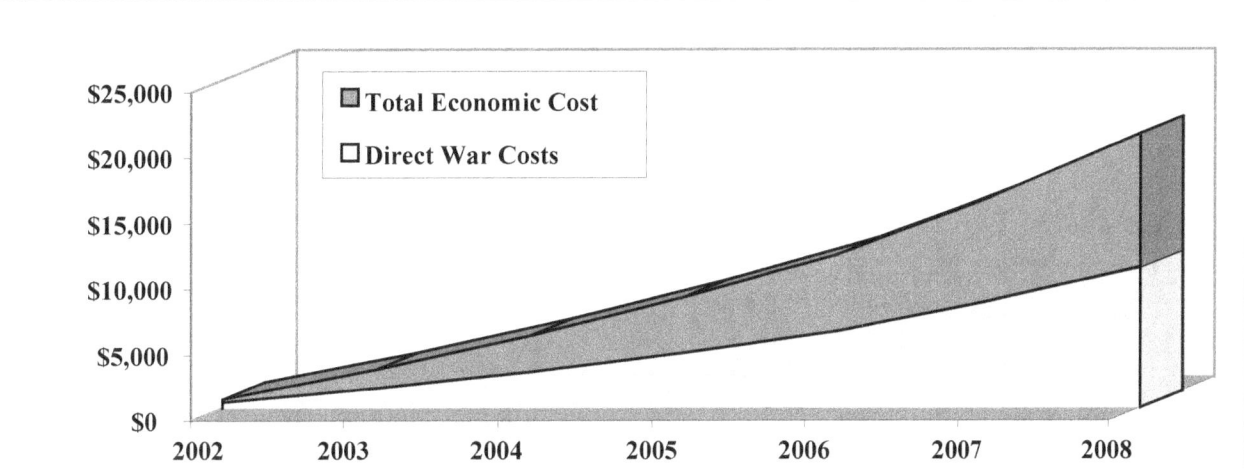

Source: CRS (2007) for prior appropriations and spending requests, JEC staff calculations. 2008 appropriation request drawn from Administration requested supplemental.

- **The war in Iraq has disrupted world oil markets leading to increased prices.** The Iraq war has occurred in a context of greatly increasing world demand for oil, as well as declining excess production capacity. Both the direct effect of the war in reducing Iraqi oil production and the indirect effect of creating greater instability in the Middle East can act to increase oil prices. Relatively small increases in oil prices can have substantial economic effects.

- **Other economic and budgetary costs have grown due to the Iraq war.** These expenditures include the costs of treating the wounded and disabled, lost productivity from those injured, potential future expansions in the size of the military made necessary by the war, the costs of repair and refit for military equipment, increases in recruitment and retention costs for the military, and economic disruptions created by the deployment of the Reserves.

The sum of the costs listed above raises the economic costs of the war from $607 billion in direct funding for the Iraq war to $1.3 trillion. If spending in Afghanistan is included, costs could reach $1.6 trillion by the close of FY 2008.

There are numerous other impacts of these wars that are not listed above and are difficult if not impossible to measure. These include the horrible human cost of the nearly 4,000 U.S. fatalities since the start of military operations in Iraq, the impact on our reputation and credibility throughout the world, and the budgetary and economic costs to other nations besides the U.S. (most notably Iraq). Finally, the debate over the broader national security impacts of the Iraq war, and related costs or benefits, is a complex issue that goes beyond the scope of this report (DoD 2007).

If We Don't Change Course, the Cost of the War will Balloon to $3.5 Trillion
The costs described above represent only the impacts of the Iraq war through the close of FY 2008 (if the President's current budget requests are approved in full). Yet at least some spending on the war will continue beyond FY 2008. Assumptions about the future course of the war are necessary to forecast the full eventual fiscal and economic impacts. Because the Administration has not been clear about future plans for U.S. forces in Iraq, these assumptions must be hypothetical.

This study mainly examines potential future costs over a ten year window, up to the year 2017, similar to the budget spending window that the CBO used. The paper focuses on a scenario corresponding to the recent statement by Secretary of Defense Robert Gates that a protracted "Korea-like" presence would be required in Iraq. This scenario involves a drawdown in Iraq troop levels of 66 percent by the year 2013, and a smaller drawdown of 33 percent in Afghanistan forces. The scenario also assumes that some active conflict with insurgents continues over the period (CBO 2007a).

In recent testimony, the nonpartisan CBO detailed Federal direct appropriations and interest costs for this scenario (CBO 2007b). These CBO estimates are used as a base for the analysis in this report. Once the full economic costs of the war are added to the approximately $2.4 trillion in Federal spending forecast under the CBO scenario, the total economic cost of the wars in Iraq and Afghanistan rise by over $1 trillion to $3.5 trillion.

Costs could far exceed these projections if the significant drawdown assumed in this scenario does not materialize. This CBO budgetary scenario projects that appropriations for the Iraq war

Table 2: Possible Economic Costs of Staying the Course (Through 2017)		
	IRAQ WAR ONLY	**IRAQ AND AFGHANISTAN**
Scenario (Troop Strength)	Gradual drawdown from 2007 level of 180,000 troops to 55,000 troops by 2013. Troop strength constant from 2013-17.	Drawdown from 2007 level of 210,000 troops to 75,000 troops by 2013. Troop strength constant from 2013-17.
Direct Appropriations*	$1.3 Trillion	$1.7 Trillion
Total Federal Spending Including Interest**	$1.9 Trillion	$2.4 Trillion
Total Economic Cost***	$2.8 Trillion	$3.5 Trillion
Costs per Family of Four	$36,900	$46,400

Budget costs in nominal dollars, flow of economic costs discounted to the relevant budget year. See Appendix B for discussion of methodology.
*Based on Administration funding request for FY 2008, CRS and CBO cost estimates of direct appropriations.
**CBO estimate from 10/24/2007 testimony to House Budget Committee (CBO 2007b).
***Based on total sum of present value costs accrued in each budgetary year over 2002-2017 period.

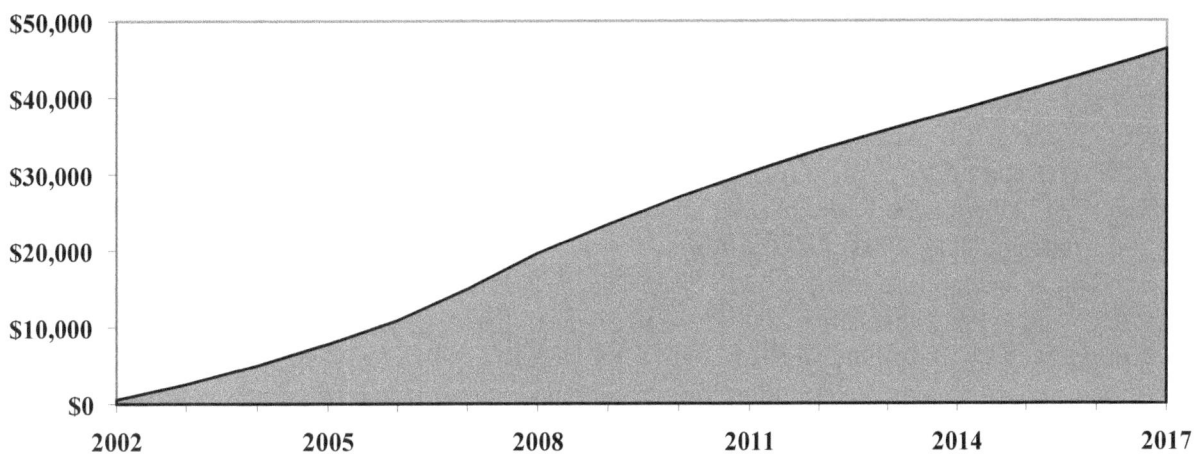

Chart 2: With No Change In Course, Total Costs Incurred Per Family Reach Almost $50,000 By 2017 (Costs For Wars In Iraq and Afghanistan)

Source: JEC staff calculation based on CRS (2007), and CBO projection of budgetary cost for "considerable drawdown" scenario.

will begin to drop significantly in 2009. But historically appropriations for the Iraq war have increased every year since the invasion, by between 12 and 40 percent annually (CRS 2007).

This report also presents costs for several alternative budgetary scenarios (Appendix A). These include costs for a rapid withdrawal from Iraq while maintaining troops in Afghanistan, and the costs to maintain current (post-surge) troop levels in Iraq for the next decade. These scenarios generate very different economic costs over the next decade. For example, maintaining post-surge troop levels in Iraq over the next ten years would result in costs of $4.5 trillion.

Each state is assumed to bear a share of the total war costs proportional to its share of the total national economy. On this basis, the report presents total state costs accrued through FY 2008, as well as potential future costs through 2017.

Part I: Taxpayer Costs of the War

This section estimates current and future taxpayer expenditures for the war, based on budgetary information from the Congressional Research Service (CRS) and Congressional Budget Office (CBO).[2] The taxpayer costs can be divided into direct appropriations for the war and interest costs for Iraq-related debt. (These interest costs are a subset of the wider economic costs calculated in this report).

DIRECT APPROPRIATIONS FOR THE WAR

Prior to the start of the Iraq war in 2003, the Bush administration estimated the total cost of the war at between $50 to $60 billion (Bumiller 2003).

The President has now requested over ten times this initial estimate just in direct appropriations for the war between FY 2003 and 2008. If the President's latest request for supplemental funding is approved, the direct expenditures authorized specifically for the Iraq war from FY 2003 to FY 2008 will total some $607 billion (CRS 2007; JEC estimates). This includes $450 billion already authorized by Congress between FY 2003 and FY 2007, plus an estimated $158 billion for Iraq from the supplemental request that the administration has made for FY 2008.[3]

Estimates of budgetary costs after 2008 depend on assumptions about the future course of the war. Appendix A of this report outlines costs for a variety of alternative scenarios, ranging from a rapid drawdown of troops to a continuation of post-surge funding and troop levels through the foreseeable future.

In the main body of this report, we focus on the CBO "considerable drawdown" scenario, which corresponds to the "Korea-like presence" recently predicted by Secretary of Defense Robert Gates. Following the war in Korea, force levels dropped to a level of between 50,000 and 60,000 troops throughout the 1960s and 1970s (Kane 2004). This scenario assumes that force levels in Iraq drop from their current level of 180,000 troops down to 55,000 by 2013, and are maintained at this level through 2017.

This level of drawdown implies that beginning in FY 2009 funding levels for Iraq will begin to drop for the first time in the history of the war. The scenario predicts direct appropriations for the

---

BOX A: HOW IS WAR IN IRAQ FUNDED?

War funding has been borrowed from the public. Since 2001, Federal government revenues as a share of Gross Domestic Product have decreased by one percent, while outlays have grown significantly and debt held by the public has increased by approximately $1.5 trillion (CBO 2007a). In this environment of growing public debt, it seems evident that the marginal dollar spent by the Federal government has been borrowed. The characterization of the Iraq war as a "war of choice" and the funding of the war through a series of off-budget emergency supplemental bills makes this even clearer.

Given the already steep fiscal demands on the Federal government, and the Administration's unwilling-ness to offer a proposal to pay for the war, it is fair to assume that the future costs of the war through 2017 will also be paid for by borrowing from the public.

The assumption that Iraq war spending is borrowed drives a number of findings in this report. These include the level of government interest costs incurred, and also the assumption that some of the borrowed funding would have remained available for additional U.S. capital investment.

---

[2] CRS 2007; CBO 2007a and 2007b. See Appendix B for full explanation of budgetary estimates.
[3] These direct budgetary costs include estimates of all of the additional spending so far for the Iraq war by the Defense Department, State Department, and the Veterans Administration, as well as reconstruction payments to Iraq.

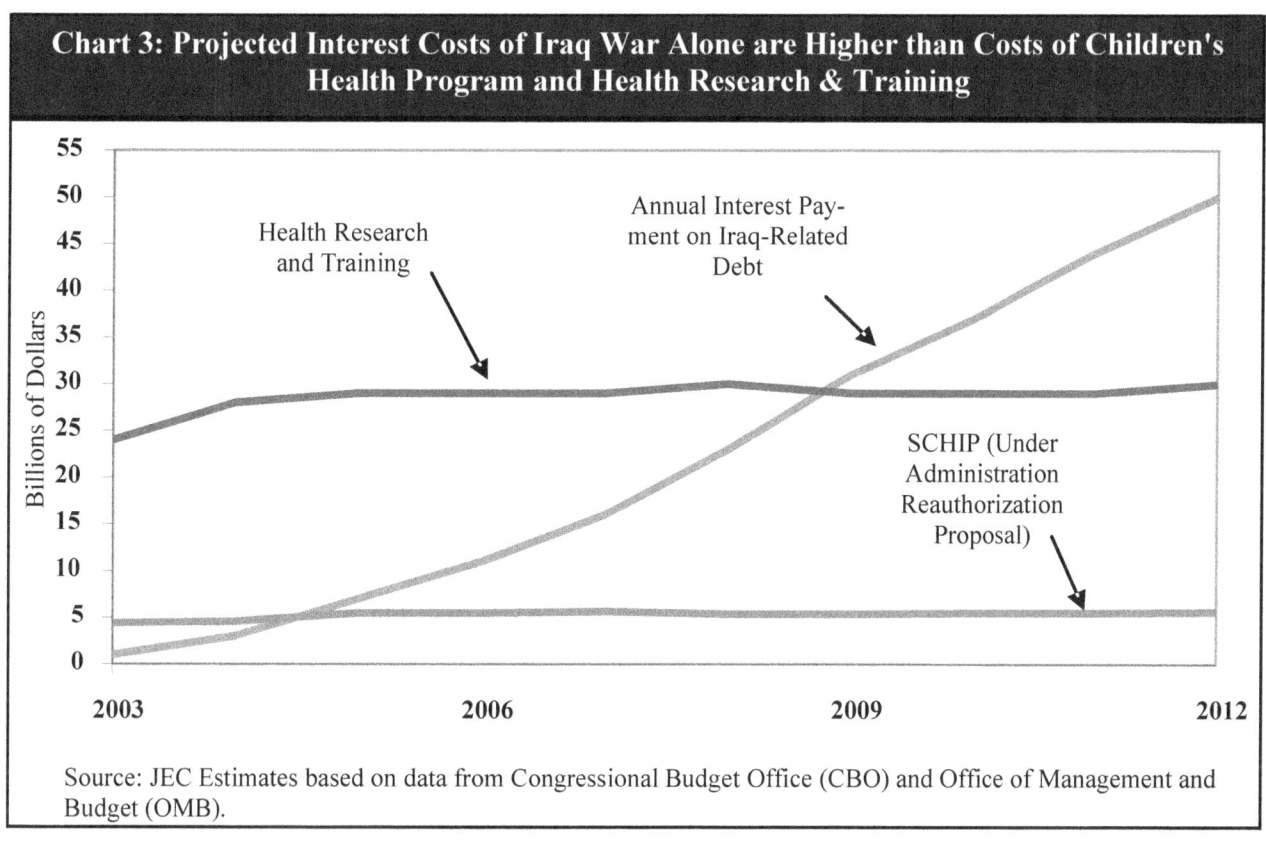

Chart 3: Projected Interest Costs of Iraq War Alone are Higher than Costs of Children's Health Program and Health Research & Training

Health Research and Training

Annual Interest Payment on Iraq-Related Debt

SCHIP (Under Administration Reauthorization Proposal)

Billions of Dollars

Source: JEC Estimates based on data from Congressional Budget Office (CBO) and Office of Management and Budget (OMB).

war drop from $135 billion in FY 2007 to less than $60 billion in FY 2013. For these reasons, the scenario should be seen as a conservative one. This CBO scenario implies an additional $690 billion in Iraq war spending through 2017 (CBO 2007a).

IRAQ RELATED DEBT AND INTEREST COSTS TO TAXPAYERS
Since war costs have been borrowed, taxpayers must also pay interest costs on the war until Iraq-related debt is retired. If the president's FY 2008 budget request is fully approved, this debt will total almost $660 billion by the close of FY 2008. It will reach almost $1.7 trillion by the close of 2017.

This debt has many economic implications, but the immediate impact on taxpayers will be the annual interest payments required. If the President's FY 2008 supplemental request for Iraq funding is passed, almost 10 percent of total Federal government interest payments in 2008 will consist of payments on the Iraq debt accumulated so far.

Interest costs on Iraq-related debt will be over $23 billion in FY 2008, and are projected to far exceed spending on programs that address key national priorities such as education and health. Chart 3 shows the current and projected future time path of interest spending through 2012. The chart shows that the annual interest costs on accumulated war debt already far exceed spending for such national priorities as health insurance for children (under the proposed Democratic SCHIP expansion recently vetoed by the President) and health research.

Under the "considerable drawdown" scenario, by the year 2017 projected interest costs on Iraq-

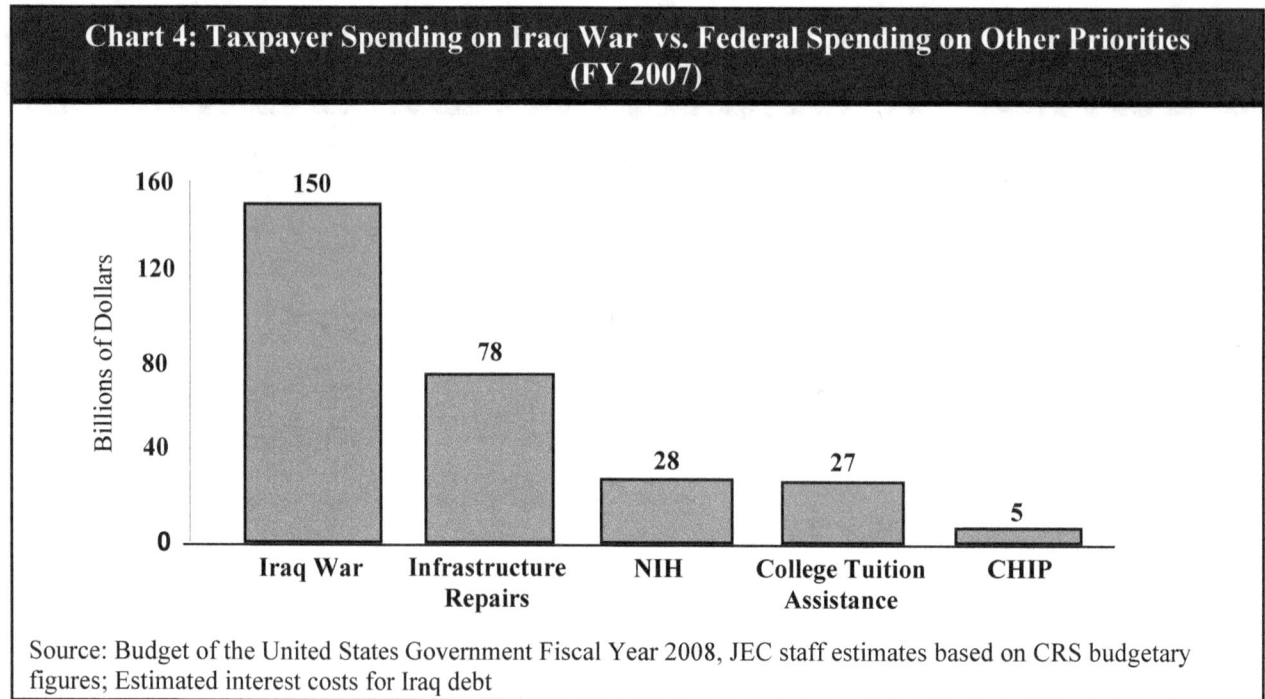

Chart 4: Taxpayer Spending on Iraq War vs. Federal Spending on Other Priorities (FY 2007)

Source: Budget of the United States Government Fiscal Year 2008, JEC staff estimates based on CRS budgetary figures; Estimated interest costs for Iraq debt

related debt will rise to $80 billion annually. The sum of interest paid on Iraq-related debt from 2003-2017 will total over $550 billion.

These interest costs are based on the assumption that interest rates will remain constant at a rate of 4.5%. Interest payments could grow significantly compared to this forecast if interest rates rise in the future.

Interest costs will continue to accrue beyond 2017 so long as the debt is not paid down. Paying down the debt will require cuts in government spending and/or increases in taxes. Alternatively, interest payments can simply be continued after 2017. Because this report projects costs accrued only through 2017, economic effects of the choices made about handling the debt after 2017 are not reflected in these estimates. It is assumed that the debt remains outstanding through the end of the forecast period.

TOTAL TAXPAYER COSTS

Total taxpayer spending is the sum of direct budget costs and interest costs. The total increase in taxpayer spending over 2003-2017 due to the Iraq war is a projected $1.9 trillion under the "considerable drawdown" scenario. If declines in future spending projected by CBO do not materialize, war spending could be substantially higher than forecast here (this issue is discussed further in Appendix A).

To put annual spending on the war in perspective, it is useful to consider the spending on other national priorities that could be funded by just one year of Iraq spending. Chart 4 shows how Iraq funding just in the recently completed 2007 fiscal year compared to spending on various other public investment priorities. The FY 2007 total of $150 billion is greater than the combined sum of Federal spending on such priorities as the nation's transportation infrastructure, health research, customs and border protection, higher education aid, environmental protection, Head Start, and the CHIP program.

Should the President's recent supplemental request be fully approved, total taxpayer spending for Iraq would be even higher in FY 2008, approximately $180 billion or $500 million per day.

Part II: Additional Economic Costs

The budgetary costs alone of the war are high. But there are many additional economic costs of the war that go beyond the direct budgetary costs. In terms of magnitude, the most significant economic costs are:

- Displacement of productive investment by U.S. companies due to increases in government borrowing.

- Interest payments to foreign capital owners for Iraq-related debt.

- Impact of the war on oil markets.

In addition, there are a number of other, smaller, costs that we discuss below. Chart 5 shows the estimated division of all economic costs from the Iraq war alone.

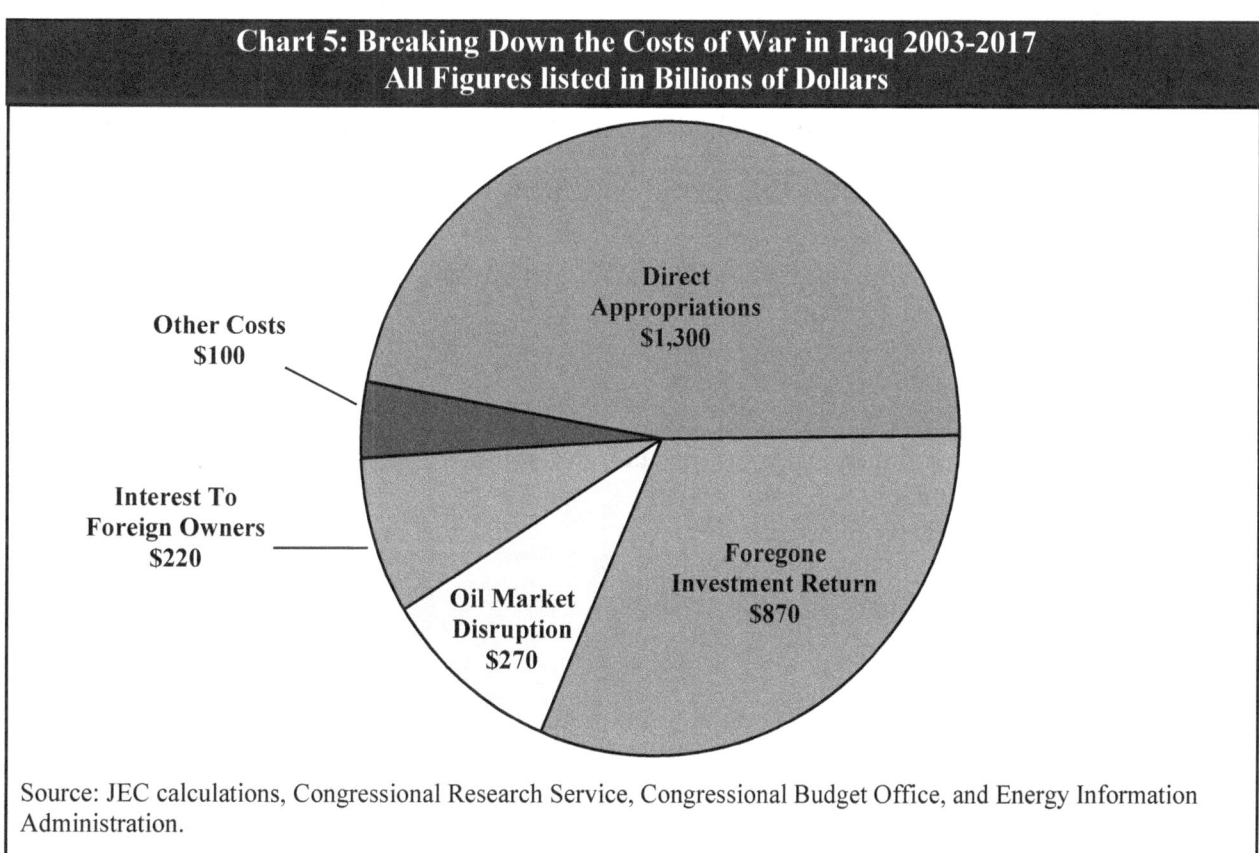

Chart 5: Breaking Down the Costs of War in Iraq 2003-2017
All Figures listed in Billions of Dollars

Other Costs $100

Interest To Foreign Owners $220

Oil Market Disruption $270

Direct Appropriations $1,300

Foregone Investment Return $870

Source: JEC calculations, Congressional Research Service, Congressional Budget Office, and Energy Information Administration.

9

THE EFFECT OF GOVERNMENT BORROWING

As discussed above, the Iraq war has likely resulted in major increases in government borrowing. There is widespread consensus among economists that such borrowing has two effects (Friedman, 2005):

- First, it reduces the growth in productive private investment in the economy. Funds are diverted from private investment to purchase government securities. This depresses the future stock of productive capital below what it otherwise would have been without the borrowing.

- Second, part of the debt is funded through borrowing from foreign capital owners. Interest payments on this debt flow out of the country and constitute an economic cost.

Both of these effects have costs to the U.S. economy. For government borrowing that fully displaces productive investment, all the future returns on this capital investment are lost. The future growth rate of the economy is reduced.

For government borrowing that is funded from world capital markets, investment is not displaced, but interest payments on this debt flow out of the economy to foreigners. (Interest payments to U.S. bond purchasers are a subset of the economic costs from displaced private investment in the U.S.).

Although there is little dispute that both of these impacts occur to some extent, the exact balance between the two effects and the proper way to evaluate them is a subject of some controversy among economists. Appendix B describes the assumptions used in this report to estimate the economic costs of Iraq-related deficit spending.

Because of these two economic impacts, the JEC estimates that Iraq-related borrowing between 2003 and 2017 will create an additional income loss of almost $1.1 trillion in present value to U.S. citizens.[4]

This loss of investment returns is the single largest cost of the Iraq war to the U.S. economy beyond the direct budgetary cost of the war itself.

IMPACT ON WORLD OIL MARKETS

Iraq is a significant oil producer, and is also located in a strategically vital region which is the center of world oil production. Since the start of the Iraq war in 2003, the price of oil has increased, from $37 per barrel (in the week prior to the war) to a recent peak of well over $90 per barrel in November 2007 (EIAa). This price increase has likely affected U.S. economic growth, and has transferred many hundreds of billions of dollars from U.S. consumers to foreign oil producers.

The war in Iraq is certainly not responsible for all of this increase. Many other factors are also affecting oil prices, including large growth in oil demand from China and India. But the consistent disruptions resulting from the war have affected oil prices.

---

[4] This is the present value of the lost returns to investments that did no take place due to the diversion of capital into Iraq war spending, as well as the present value of post-tax returns to investments that were funded with foreign capital. The assumptions used to generate this estimate are further described in Appendix B.

The Iraq War and Oil Prices

The war in Iraq has two potential effects on world oil markets. The first is a direct effect, stemming from disruption in Iraqi oil exports to the world market. The second is an indirect psychological effect.

The direct effect can be examined by considering Iraqi oil exports compared to capacity. The Energy Information Administration has stated that current Iraq production of roughly 2 million barrels per day (BPD) is "down from around 2.6 million BPD of production and a nameplate capacity of 2.8 to 3 million BPD in pre-invasion January, 2003." (EIA 2007c).

Taking the EIA estimate of 2.6 million BPD of actual pre-war production, the reduction in direct Iraqi oil production has ranged from roughly 1.3 million BPD (in the invasion year of 2003) to about 600,000 BPD today. These shortfalls likely impact world oil prices. As a CBO report discussing oil market developments from 2003-2006 stated:

"Today, however, worldwide production is close to its short-term limits. As a result, oil markets appear much more vulnerable than before to an interruption in supply or a rapid increase in demand. Even the threat of a reduction in supply of a few hundred thousand barrels a day causes sharp fluctuations in prices" (CBO 2006).

As a rule of thumb, the Department of Energy estimates that a 1 percent decline in world oil supply generally leads to about a 10 percent rise in prices (EIA 2004, GAO 2006). Using this rule leads to the prediction that shortfalls of the levels discussed above might be expected to increase oil prices by around 15% in 2003, and 7-9% in 2004-2007. Because of rising prices, this percentage increase creates a consistent rise in the price of oil of roughly $5.00 per barrel.

The Iraq war could have a second, indirect effect on oil prices if events in Iraq have led to concerns about wider regional conflict, or increases in terrorism in the region that could affect oil fields. These kinds of fears would cause investors to bid up the price of oil on futures markets, and increase the stockpiles of oil they hold against an emergency.

BOX B: MARKET PSYCHOLOGY

A recent CRS report on world oil prices singled out the Iraq war as having an important impact on market psychology:

"The war in Iraq has contributed to high oil prices in different ways as events have progressed. The predominant effect of the conflict on oil prices has been an increase in uncertainty. During the early stages of the conflict, concerns about a possible disruption of oil supply out of the Persian Gulf and disruption of Iraqi production due to military operations were prominent....Later, market uncertainty revolved around the ability of Iraq to export oil in the midst of political transition in which pipeline and other oil facilities were attacked by hostile groups within the country. Uncertainty with respect to terrorist attacks, both in Iraq, and spilling over to other Gulf nations, including Saudi Arabia, continue to unsettle the oil market and contribute to a "fear factor" being built into the price of oil." (CRS, 2005)

It seems likely that indirect psychological factors related to the Iraq war did contribute to increases in oil prices in 2003, and been one of several factors contributing to oil price volatility since then.

It is hard to quantify the size of this effect on prices. But it seems clear that the Iraq war has been one factor contributing to a generally unsettled state of oil markets over the past several years. This is due to the combination of the timing of the war during a period when world oil markets have been under unusual stress from increased demand, and the psychological effects of the increased geopolitical uncertainty due to the war. The combination of direct and psychological effects helps to support the price effect discussed above.

The Economic Impact of Higher Oil Prices

What impact does this increase in oil prices have on the U.S. economy? There are two separable effects. The first impact is a direct transfer to wealth from U.S. consumers to foreign oil producers driven by the rise in oil prices. This estimated effect can be counteracted somewhat by reductions in oil consumption by consumers or if foreign oil profits are spent in the U.S. JEC estimates find that from 2003-2008 this effect will transfer approximately $124 billion from U.S. oil consumers to foreign producers.[5]

Most economists agree that there is likely a further impact of oil price increases on the economy. Beyond any direct transfer effect, oil price shocks reduce economic growth, due to reductions in consumer demand and various adjustment costs by industries that use oil. However, there is substantial controversy over the exact size of the effect. It is generally agreed that these economic impacts of oil price increases have declined in today's economy as compared to the 1970s (Nordhaus 2007). Estimates using macroeconomic simulation models often find small costs (CBO 2006). However, estimates based on examining the actual past responses of the U.S. economy to oil price changes often find much larger impacts, ranging from five to fifteen times those found in model-based estimates.

It seems likely that the impact varies substantially depending on the exact type of oil price shock and how it is sustained, with sharp, surprising increases in oil prices having the largest negative effects on growth, and slow and expected increases having smaller or potentially no effect (Li, Ni, and Ratti 1995; Huntington 2005). But the Iraq war has produced a consistent series of surprises as the insurgency has grown, unforeseen interference with oil fields has continued, and new political disruptions have occurred (such as tensions with Iran and conflict between Kurdistan and Turkey). As discussed above, this has taken place in an environment of limited spare production capacity, and new peaks in world oil prices almost every year.

For this reason, the analysis assumes that Iraq-related oil price increases have had a wider economic effect. In particular, the analysis assumes a consistent effect throughout the 2003-2008 period that is proportional to the roughly $5 per barrel price increase described above. However, no further economic impacts from rising oil prices are assumed for 2009 or after.[6] The magnitude of

---

[5] This is based on the assumption of a − .1 elasticity for oil consumption by U.S. energy consumers and a recycling of 10% of foreign oil revenues into the U.S. economy.

[6] Such additional impacts in 2009 and following years are in quite possible, but since they cannot be reasonably predicted they have not been included in the analysis.

the GDP impact is assumed to be moderate to low. It is consistent with a wide range of recent studies.[7]

Under these assumptions, oil price increases from 2003-2008 due to the Iraq war reduced total U.S. income GDP by a total of approximately $274 billion, a direct transfer of about $124 billion and a further GDP effect of $150 billion.

OTHER ECONOMIC IMPACTS

There are numerous other costs of the wars in Iraq and Afghanistan that are not reflected in budget estimates. However, these impacts are even more difficult to estimate than the costs discussed above. They are also generally somewhat smaller than the impacts discussed above. The JEC estimates that a fuller accounting of these impacts would add at least $110 billion to the total future costs of the two wars.

The Impact of Wounds and Disabilities

One such economic impact is the costs of care for wounded and disabled veterans. Some 28,000 troops have been wounded in Iraq through October 2007 and almost half could not be returned to duty within 72 hours (DoD 2007). Should the war continue through 2017, it is reasonable to expect additional casualties.

Estimates of the costs of disability compensation and medical care for these injured veterans vary significantly. CBO has estimated the direct Federal cost of disability payments and medical care for Iraq War veterans over the 2003-2017 period (CBO 2007b). This estimate of approximately $10 billion is included in the budgetary estimates given above. The cost rises to $13 billion when Afghanistan veterans are included.

Other estimates of the entire eventual economic costs of disability among all Iraq war veterans are far higher than CBO, running as high as several hundred billion dollars (Bilmes 2007). But these estimates may not fully separate out the incremental impact of the Iraq war. Some veterans would likely have incurred disabilities during their army service even if they served during peacetime. Further study is needed to determine the full increment in injury and disability to veterans serving in wartime as opposed to peacetime.

But it is still likely that the CBO estimate underestimates the total economic cost experienced due to injuries or disabilities created by the war. Since the CBO cost estimate runs only through 2017, it does not include the full lifetime cost of care for these injured veterans. In addition, CBO may have underestimated the number of veterans not wounded in action who will eventually seek disability benefits or medical care due to war-related health issues. Finally, there is evidence that veterans disability benefits do not always fully compensate for earnings losses due to certain conditions.

---

[7] Specifically, the assumption is that a 10 percent rise in oil prices reduces GDP by two-tenths of one percentage point. This produces GDP impacts consistent with the recent Global Insight simulation of a $10 rise in oil prices (Huntington, 2005). It is smaller than the effect found in a recent literature survey by Jones, Leiby and Paik (2004) and the most recent study by Hamilton (2004), who both estimate an impact of between five and sixth tenths of a percentage point of GDP per ten percent rise in oil prices. However, this GDP impact is somewhat larger than that estimated by the Congressional Budget Office (2006).

The types of injuries and disabilities sustained in the war add to the uncertainty about future medical costs. As battlefield medical care has advanced, the number of seriously injured soldiers who survive their wounds has increased. Iraq therefore has a higher ratio of wounded to fatalities than previous wars, and the severity of wounds has correspondingly increased (CBO 2007d). For example, about 800 wounded soldiers have been injured severely enough to require amputations.

In addition, the widespread use of improvised explosive devices by insurgents has led to a high incidence of traumatic brain injury (TBI) among both wounded troops and those soldiers who survive explosions without other injuries. A recent estimate is that 10 to 20 percent of returning soldiers who believed themselves to be healthy had in fact experienced mild to moderate TBI (PCCWW 2007). The future potential health impacts and costs of TBI (especially in its mild to moderate form) are not yet well understood.

Post-traumatic stress disorder (PTSD) is another important health issue related to the Iraq conflict. This psychological reaction to traumatic stress appears to affect a substantial number of returning soldiers. Estimates indicate that between 10 and 20 percent of returning soldiers show at least some symptoms of the disorder (Hoge et. al 2007; PCCWW 2007). Some 40,000 returning soldiers have already received an official diagnosis (CBO 2007d). Research on the economic effects of PTSD indicates that it can lead to substantial reductions in earnings and employment capacity (Veterans Commission 2007; Savoca and Rosenheck 2000). Advances in treatment have been made, but there is still a great deal of uncertainty about the future economic impacts of this disorder and the number of veterans who will eventually be affected.

The JEC estimates that these factors are likely to add $25 billion to the total economic costs of injury in the Iraq war, beyond the 2003-2017 costs projected by CBO:

- A projection of the present value of the lifetime disability and medical care costs for injured veterans beyond 2017 gives a result of approximately $11 to $15 billion in additional expenses for the Iraq war.[8] When the cost of the Afghanistan war is included, this rises to about $13 to $17 billion.

- There are additional economic costs of injury that are not reflected in VA disability benefits or medical expenses. One of these is earnings losses that are not fully compensated for by disability benefits. As estimate of earnings losses related to PTSD alone finds an additional $10 billion in lost earnings to Iraq veterans that are not reflected in VA benefits.[9]

- The families of injured veterans expend considerable time and effort to provide care for their loved ones. This can have significant economic costs. A survey by the Dole-Shalala commission found that almost 20% of injured veterans stated a family member had to quit a job to provide care for them. This implies additional economic costs potentially as high as $1 billion.

- Future disabilities resulting from past wars have typically been underestimated early in the conflict (Veterans Commission 2007). However, at this time it is very difficult to project what level of additional disabilities beyond CBO forecasts may result from the Iraq war.

---

[8] Based on projecting the present value of CBO disability and medical care costs for the year 2017 over an additional 30 years, with an adjustment for the proportion estimated to come from Iraq. The exact figure depends on what the starting year of discounting is; discounting to 2008 dollars produces the $9 billion figure, while discounting to 2017 dollars yields a $12 billion cost.

[9] See Appendix B. The cost rises to $12 billion when Afghanistan veterans are included.

These costs do not represent the total cost of injuries and disabilities to veterans. Instead they represent only the additional economic costs not already included in estimated Federal spending on injured veterans and should be understood as highly conservative.

Additional Military Costs

Between 2003 and 2006 alone, the cost of retention bonuses and re-enlistment incentives for the Army, Marines, Reserve, and National Guard have skyrocketed, rising by $800 million annually (Associated Press 2007). If these increased costs stayed constant over the 2003-17 period, they would add $13 billion to military budgets over the period. These costs are not reflected in the budgetary costs previously mentioned.

The military and other sources have also estimated a variety of potential repair and reset costs for replacing and repairing equipment damaged in the Iraq conflict. Iraq-related reset costs in the FY 2007 military budget alone totaled some $27 billion (DoD 2007). This figure is included in the budgetary costs already totaled previously.

However, the Department of Defense estimates that approximately $40 billion in reset costs will be required after withdrawal from Iraq (DoD 2007). These future costs are not included in the budget estimates described previously, and therefore they are added under "additional costs".[10]

Finally, the Administration has requested a significant long-term increase in the number of enlisted personnel in the Army and Marine Corps (CBO 2007e). This increase will eventually total 65,000 additional troops for the Army and 27,000 additional for the Marine Corps. The CBO calculated costs of approximately $17 billion annually for this expansion between 2008 and 2012. But these costs were not included in CBO tallies of the costs of the Iraq or Afghanistan wars, since the Administration has not justified this proposed increase in the size of the military solely with reference to these wars (CBO 2007e).

However, it seems clear that the wars in Iraq and Afghanistan have contributed to the need for an expansion in the size of the military. For this reason, the JEC analysis adds one-quarter of the estimated cost of this increase in military forces (or $4.25 billion annually) as an additional cost of the war beginning in 2009. This is a conservative estimate of the level of increase in military forces that could be required by these wars.

These additional military costs add approximately $85 to $90 billion to total war costs for Iraq and Afghanistan combined. Based on the split in force levels between Afghanistan and Iraq going forward, the report assigns 80 percent of this total, or about $70 billion, to the Iraq war.

Costs of National Guard and Reserve Deployments

Some half a million of the National Guard and Reserve have so far been deployed in Iraq. Some of the costs of this mobilization are reflected in government budgetary costs. But some are not, including the disruption for employers created by the loss of staff.

---

[10] CBO has raised some question over how much of the repair, reset, and reconditioning costs related to Iraq are in fact purchases of new equipment that was not made necessary by the Iraq war (CBO 2007f). However, in this report we accept the DOD estimate.

ADDITIONAL (UNQUANTIFIED) IMPACTS OF THE IRAQ WAR

This report does not attempt to quantify any demand-side macroeconomic effects of war spending on the economy. Because the war began in the wake of the 2001 recession, some of the war spending could have worked to close a small part of the recessionary gap between potential and realized production. However, the bulk of the war spending took place well after the recession and any additional demand-side macroeconomic effects (difficult to estimate in any case) are not likely to be large with respect to the ongoing effects of war spending on the economy.

The over 3,800 American fatalities that have resulted from the war so far are a tragedy that is difficult to quantify in economic terms. These losses can be seen as creating a direct economic effect of many billions of dollars in lost productivity and creativity for the nation. To this must be added the psychological costs of the loss to loved ones, families, and communities. The national security and foreign policy impacts of the war are beyond the scope of this study. Finally, the impact of the war on the nation of Iraq is also beyond the scope of the report.

Part III: State-by-State Cost Estimates for the War

War costs can also be expressed in terms of the costs to each U.S. state. Table 3 shows the budgetary costs and total economic costs divided between all fifty states, in proportion to each state's share of the Federal tax burden. Each state's share of total economic costs is also shown, divided in proportion to their share of national GDP. (States will incur the full economic costs of the war in proportion to their share of the economy). State shares of total costs vary from $358 billion in California to $5.5 billion in Wyoming.

Conclusion

The direct appropriations alone devoted to the Iraq war are staggering. President Bush has already requested Iraq war appropriations over ten times his original pre-war cost estimate. The President's appropriations request for FY 2008 for Iraq alone exceeds total U.S. state, local, and Federal spending on our entire surface transportation system. Yet this report has demonstrated that the indirect costs to the American economy are roughly twice these direct appropriations.

If the President's supplemental funding request for FY 2008 is approved, the accrued costs to the economy accrued through 2008 for the wars in Iraq and Afghanistan through FY 2008 will exceed $1.6 trillion. This is over $20,000 per family of four.

Yet the costs that we will incur if the war continues are far greater. Even assuming the optimistic scenario of a significant drawdown in troop strength and no further impacts on oil markets, a continuation of the war through 2017 will lead to total economic costs for Iraq and Afghanistan of some $3.5 trillion over the 2003-17 period under the considerable drawdown scenario.

Map: States Bear Billions in Iraq War Costs
Total Economic Costs of the Iraq War 2003-2017

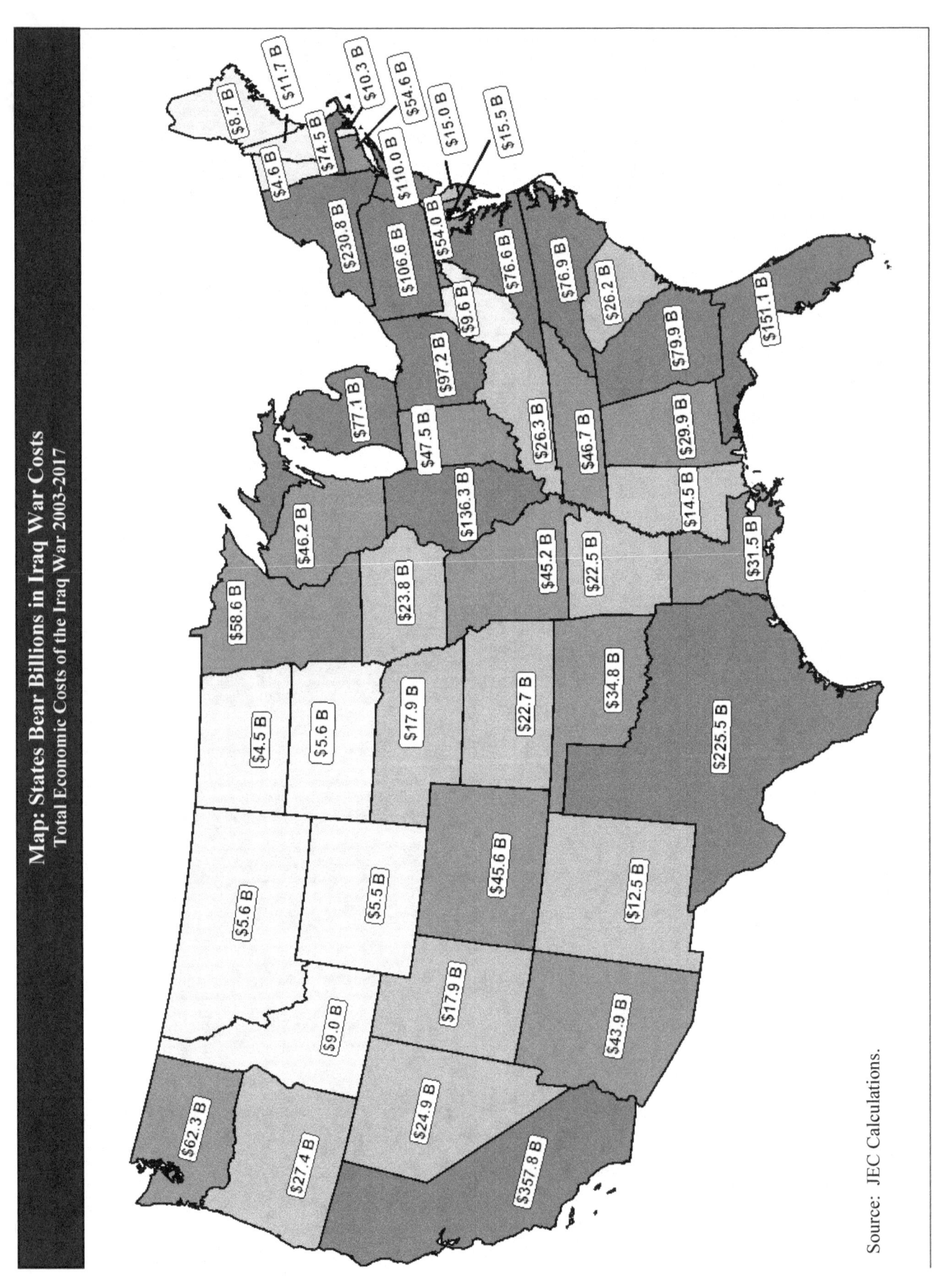

Source: JEC Calculations.

We have already experienced massive economic costs due to our failed strategy in Iraq. The nation will experience even more significant costs if we do not change course.

The Economic Burden of The Iraq War

The economic costs calculated in this report are a conservative estimate of the potential costs to the U.S. economy if we do not change course in Iraq. This study does not include such unquantifiable impacts as the cost of thousands of U.S. fatalities in these wars or the effect of the Iraq war on U.S. international prestige and security. The report assumes no oil market impacts of a continued Iraq occupation beyond 2008. The report uses conservative economic assumptions throughout, especially for the economic burden of injuries and disabilities resulting from the war. Finally, the report focuses on costs for a future scenario that assumes a substantial reduction in troop levels and budgetary costs of the war.

Despite these conservative assumptions, the economic cost of the war so far is already well over a trillion dollars. The combined costs of the wars in Iraq and Afghanistan is forecast to climb to some $3.5 trillion over the next decade if the occupation of Iraq is maintained. This will be true even if a considerable drawdown takes place and annual direct appropriations for the Iraq war decline by more than half over the next five years. By any measure, the economic costs of continuing our current course in Iraq would be enormous.

Appendix A: Costs of Alternative Scenarios

War costs through 2007 can be directly calculated. In this study, war costs for FY 2008 were estimated by taking the figures in the President's supplemental spending request, as allocated by the Congressional Research Service.

Cost projections for FY 2009-17 require forecasting the future course of the war. The main body of the report focused on the CBO's "moderate drawdown" scenario to project future costs. This "moderate drawdown" scenario assumes a 64% drop in the number of troops in Iraq by 2013, and constant force levels from 2013-17. The scenario implies a sharp decline in war costs beginning in 2009.

This appendix supplements this scenario with two others. The first is a "sharp drawdown" scenario under which forces in Iraq are rapidly reduced to 10,000 by 2010, and withdrawn altogether by 2011. This scenario corresponds roughly to withdrawal scenarios advanced by House Democrats. The underlying budgetary figures are based on CBO fiscal estimates for a sharp drawdown scenario, with costs in later years assumed to occur entirely in Afghanistan and not in Iraq. FY 2008 funding is assumed to be somewhat lower than the President's request. The future costs for disabilities, as well as additional military costs such as recruitment, force expansion, and repair, are also assumed to be a total of $35 billion lower under this scenario.

The second is a "no drawdown" or "status quo" scenario which assumes post-surge cost levels for the war continue throughout the budget window until 2017. This scenario corresponds to an indefinite continuation of the war. To perform this estimate, JEC staff adopted a CBO estimate of FY 2009 costs. At $121 billion per year, this estimated spending would still be over $10 billion lower than Iraq war spending in FY 2007, and over $30 billion lower than FY 2008 spending will be if the President's supplemental is approved. (It would thus represent the first annual decline in Iraq spending since the start of the war). The "no drawdown" scenario then assumes this spending stays constant in real terms (adjusted for a 2% inflation level) through 2017. This reflects a continued commitment of 155,000 troops to the occupation of Iraq. The costs for disabilities, as well as additional military costs such as recruitment, force expansion, and repair, are also assumed to be a total of $35 billion higher under this scenario.

Table A-1 and Chart A-1 show force levels and total costs in Iraq and Afghanistan for all three scenarios. Because such a large amount of war costs have already been incurred, all of the scenarios show large total expenses for the war. (For example, all three scenarios require continued interest payments on war-related debt accumulated so far). However, the difference between the "sharp drawdown" and "no drawdown" scenarios amounts to a savings of approximately $2 trillion in total economic costs incurred between 2003 and 2017.

Table A-1: Descriptions and Costs of Alternative Future Scenarios				
Scenario	**Troop Levels in Iraq and Afghanistan**		**Estimated Total Economic Costs (2003-2017)**	
	2007	**2008-2017**	**Iraq and Afghanistan**	**Iraq Only**
No Drawdown (Status Quo)	210,000 (180,000 in Iraq)	Reduction to 180,000 troops total (155,000 in Iraq) by FY 2009. No further reduction.	$4.5 Trillion	$3.5 Trillion
Considerable Drawdown (Korea-like Presence)	210,000 (180,000 in Iraq)	Gradual reduction to 75,000 troops total (55,000 in Iraq) by 2013. This force strength maintained through 2017.	$3.5 Trillion	$2.8 Trillion
Sharp Drawdown (House Democratic Plan)	210,000 (180,000 in Iraq)	Rapid reduction to 30,000 troops total (10,000 in Iraq) by 2010. Full withdrawal from Iraq after 2010; 20,000 troops maintained in Afghanistan	$2.6 Trillion	$1.7 Trillion

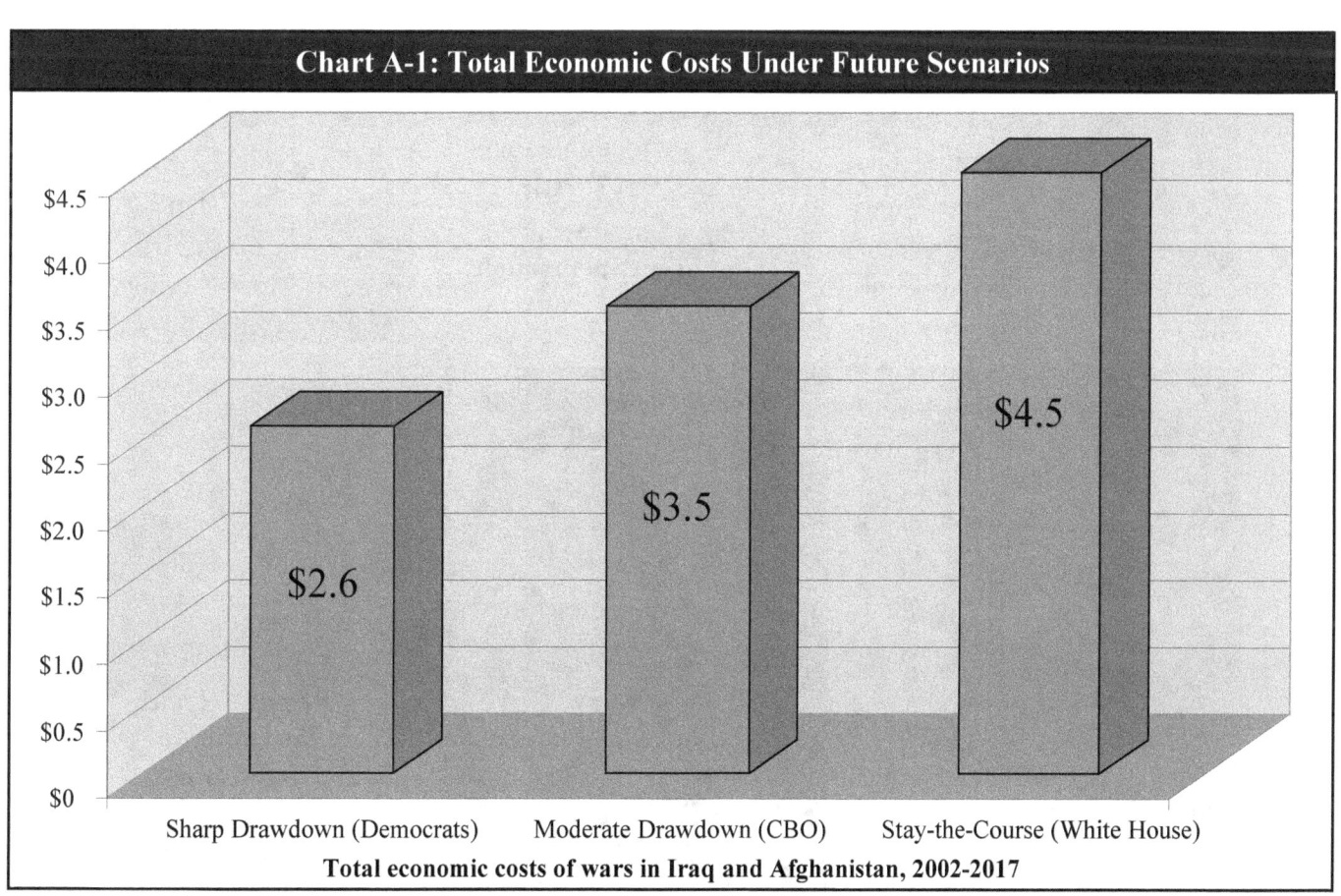

Chart A-1: Total Economic Costs Under Future Scenarios

Total economic costs of wars in Iraq and Afghanistan, 2002-2017

Table A-2 Alternative Ways to Spend the $432 Million We Spend In Iraq Every Day		
	Current Enrollment per Year	**Potential Enrollment**
People Insured through SCHIP	6,400,000	513,000
Head Start Participants	909,200	58,000
Pell Grants	5,000,000	163,700
Border Patrol Agents	12,300	10,700
State and Local Police	580,700	14,200
Teachers	6,800,000	9,300

Sources: Expect More Data (expectmore.gov) and Congressional Budget Office Data (cbo.gov)

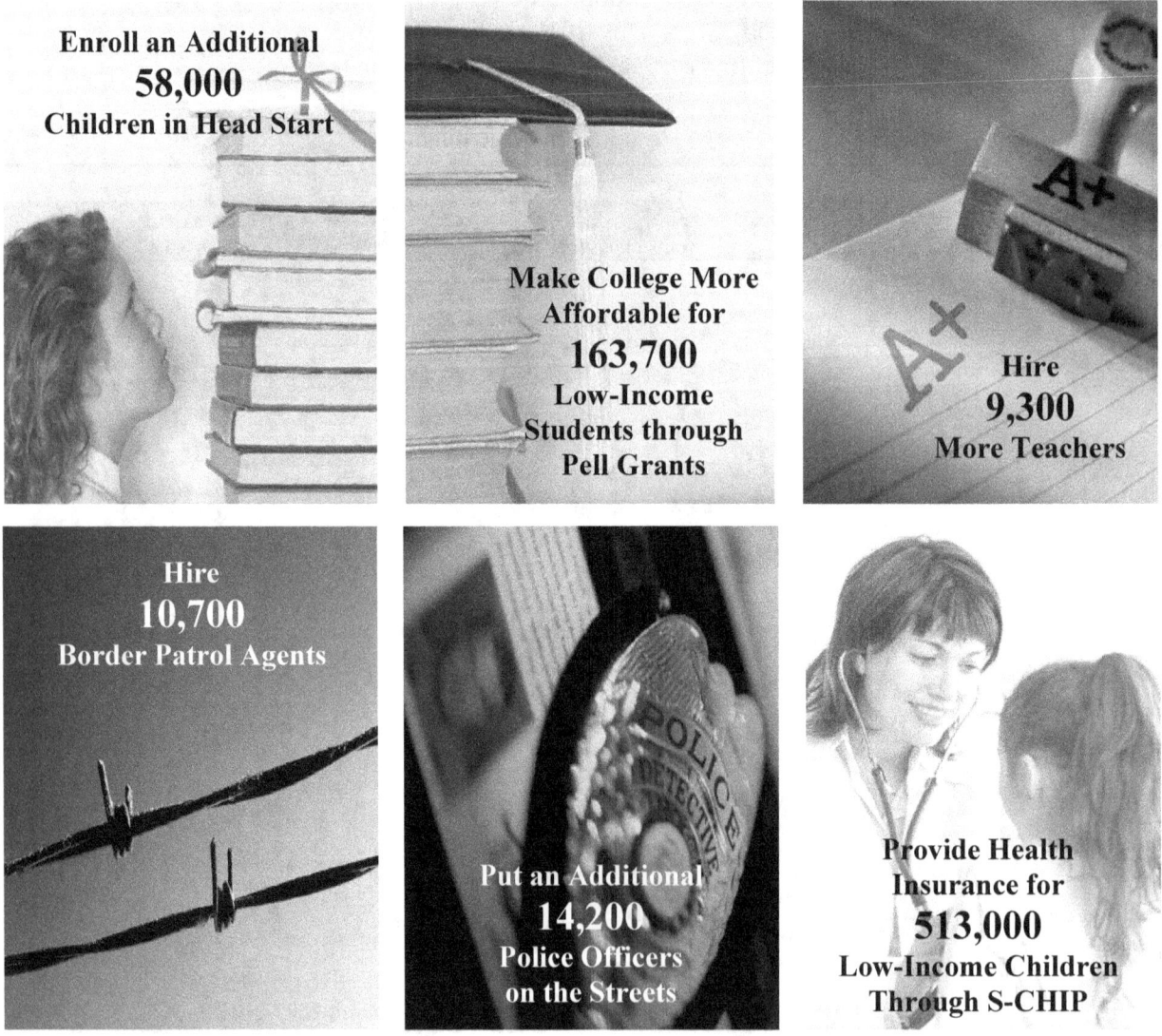

Enroll an Additional **58,000** Children in Head Start

Make College More Affordable for **163,700** Low-Income Students through Pell Grants

Hire **9,300** More Teachers

Hire **10,700** Border Patrol Agents

Put an Additional **14,200** Police Officers on the Streets

Provide Health Insurance for **513,000** Low-Income Children Through S-CHIP

Appendix B: Methodology

The Economic Cost Concept

Conceptually, economic costs in this paper are the sum of all costs to taxpayers, plus additional costs to Americans that are not reflected in government budgets. To be a valid measure of total costs, this method requires the assumption that costs to taxpayers exactly reflect the true resource cost of the goods or services being purchased by government.

Of course, this assumption may not be completely true. Some government costs may include, for example, profits in excess of normal rates of return for government contractors. In many analyses of overall economic costs these profits would be scored as transfers and not costs at all (they would act as offsetting benefits to government costs). But in this case the results of adopting such a technique would be misleading and counterintuitive. For example, if profits were scored as transfers, this would imply that cases of contractor fraud in which Americans earned large profits by cheating the government would reduce the overall costs of the Iraq war to the taxpayer.

Because of the assumption that government costs reflect true resource costs, those resource costs that appear in government budgets are not counted twice. To take one example, when disability payments to injured veterans make up for part or all of their lost earnings, these lost earnings are not counted again in economic costs.

Calculations of Budgetary Spending

Figures from the Congressional Research Service (CRS) were used to determine the total amounts expended on the Iraq and Afghanistan wars through the close of 2007, and also in the President's 2008 supplemental request (CRS 2007).[11]

Budgetary figures for 2009 and after were drawn from testimony by the Congressional Budget Office (CBO). These figures are drawn from Tables 5 through 7 of Robert Sunshine's testimony to the House Budget Committee in July, 2007. They are increased by 10% to reflect higher levels of spending than expected at that time. (This increase is explained in CBO director Peter Orszag's testimony before the House Budget Committee in October 2007). The scenario used in the main body of the report corresponds to Scenario 2 in this CBO testimony, with the 12-month sustained surge option assumed. Based on discussions with CBO staff, 80% of these budgetary costs are assumed to be incurred in the Iraq war.

The two other scenarios described in Appendix A also draw on these CBO budgetary figures, but are modified as described in Appendix A.

Accrued Costs of Foregone Investment

The accrued costs of foregone investment related to borrowed funds are estimated using a shadow cost of capital approach. This approach converts lost investment into the present value of a stream of future consumption. There is substantial agreement that this approach is theoretically correct (Cline 1992). However, there are a variety of methods to calculate the shadow cost. Some methods can have results that depend heavily on assumptions (Lyon 1990).

This report uses a comparatively stable and conservative means for calculating the shadow cost of capital, that is less fragile to assumptions than other methods. The description and justification for the technique is outlined in Cline (1992). This method involves summing the real present value of total returns to capital

---

[11] These figures differ slightly from CBO figures, as CBO is willing to leave some costs unallocated to either Iraq or Afghanistan while CRS analysts allocate the entire amount to a specific war.

over a 15 year time horizon. Capital investment returns are calculated using the marginal pre-tax return to private investment, and discounted by the social rate of time preference. All of the capital return is assumed to be consumed, except for whatever share is necessary to compensate for depreciation. The key assumptions involved are:

1. The amount of borrowed money that represents displaced capital investment. This study assumes 60% of Iraq-related government borrowing represents displaced investment. The other 40% is assumed to be replaced by foreign investors. This figure is directly drawn from an estimate of the economic impact of deficits by the Bush Administration Council of Economic Advisors in 2003 (CEA 2003).

2. The pre-tax real marginal rate of return to capital. This report assumes a 7% real rate of return on capital, net of depreciation. This is the standard assumption that the Office of Management requests that agencies use as the alternative return to capital used in government expenditures (OMB 1992).[12]

3. The social rate of time preference, or discount rate. This report assumes a 3% discount rate. The inflation-adjusted cost of Treasury borrowing in recent years has been between 2 and 3% (OMB). The use of this Treasury borrowing rate is also recommended by OMB when using the shadow price of capital approach. The rate is higher than the standard 2% rate used by CBO. (OMB 1992; Kohyama 2006).

The economic costs of foregone investment are then summed in the following manner:

1. The increase in Federal borrowing each year is calculated using assumptions about the fraction of appropriations that are spent in each year.

2. Sixty percent of increased borrowing is assumed to displace capital.

3. The discounted real present value of the displaced capital is summed over a 15 year time horizon.

4. The present value of costs are counted as accrued in the year in which the Iraq-related borrowing took place.

The stream of foregone investment earnings is discounted to the year in which the borrowing took place. This is done to match economic costs with the reported budget figures from CBO reports and testimony (CBO 2007b, c). The costs in the body of the report can therefore be understood as describing future losses to the economy over the entire 2003-2017 period.

Interest Payments to Foreign Creditors
The 40% of borrowing that does not represent displaced capital is assumed to be borrowed from foreign purchasers of debt. Outflows of interest to these foreign creditors represent an economic loss. Therefore, each year 40% of payments on Iraq-related debt are counted as an economic loss. Based on discussions with CBO staff, interest payments are calculated at a 4.5% interest rate.

Other Costs: Medical Costs
As discussed in the main body of the report, CBO has attempted to forecast Federal medical and disability costs for war-related injuries up to the year 2017. This report adds on the present value cost of a continuation of these medical and disability costs for a 30-year period, discounted at a 3% rate. Medical costs are assumed to decline at a rate of roughly 10% per year due to the healing of injuries and illnesses. Disability costs remain constant.

---

[12] Other estimates are higher; for example, Gomme, Ravikumar, and Rupert (2006) estimate 7.7% as the average of the real marginal return over the 1950-2001 period. This would result in a larger amount of lost investment.

The report also adds on a cost of lost earnings for one sample war-related disability, post-traumatic stress disorder (PTSD). The majority of lost earnings costs due to war injuries are assumed to already be counted in VA disability payments, which compensate for such earnings losses and are included in budgetary costs. However, a recent study commissioned by the Veterans Commission on the adequacy of disability benefits found that such benefits only compensate about 80 percent of the earnings losses due to mental disabilities such as PTSD (Christensen et. al 2007).

The report assumes that 15 percent of serving veterans over the 2002-17 period will eventually experience PTSD (Hoge et. al 2007; PCCWW, 2007). The report also assumes that they will experience earnings losses of roughly 20 percent (Savoca and Rosenheck 2000). Finally, the assumption is made that the average present value of lifetime earnings for a veteran absent PTSD is $2 million. (This estimate is based on inflation-adjusted results from civilians from Day and Newburger 2002). The $10 billion figure in the text was calculated based on these assumptions combined with the average under compensation from VA benefits discussed above.

Discounting Costs Over The Budget Window

This report discounts war costs to each specific budget year. For example, the lost future consumption due to debt-related displaced investment is discounted to the year the money was borrowed. Likewise, the future costs of disabilities and injuries for veterans are discounted to approximately the estimated year of the injury. However, costs are not discounted across budget years. This was done to maintain comparability with actual budget figures and future CBO budgetary estimates, which are not discounted.

An alternative method would be to discount all war costs to some specific budget year, such as FY 2008. Discounting and deflating total costs to real FY 2008 dollars does reduce the overall cost of the Iraq war between 2003 and 2017. However, the effect is not large. This is partly because discounting to 2008 increases costs incurred in FY 2003-2007. It is also because under the "moderate drawdown" scenario the bulk of total costs are incurred in years close to 2008.

As an example of the effect of discounting, discounting all costs to real FY 2008 dollars at a 3% discount rate and an assumed 2% inflation rate reduces the total costs of the Iraq war under the "moderate drawdown" scenario from $2.77 trillion to $2.58 trillion. The combined costs of the wars in Iraq and Afghanistan are reduced from $3.48 trillion to $3.25 trillion. Costs of the war between 2002 and 2008 alone would of course be increased by this exercise.

Bibliography

Bilmes, Linda, 2007. "Soldiers Returning from Iraq and Afghanistan: The Long-term Costs Providing Veterans Medical Care and Disability Benefits." Working Paper, Harvard University.

Bumiller, Elizabeth, 2003. "The Cost of War." *The New York Times*, p. 4.2.

Christensen et al, 2007. "Final Report for the Veterans' Disability Benefits Commission: Compensation, Survey Results, and Selected Topics." The CNA Corporation, CRM D0016570.A2.

Cline, William R, 1992. *The Economics of Global Warming*. Peterson Institute for International Economics.

Congressional Research Service (CRS), 2007. "The Cost of Iraq, Afghanistan, and Other Global War on Terror Operations Since 9/11."

-- 2005. "World Oil Demand and its Effect on Oil Prices."

Congressional Budget Office (CBO), 2007a. "The Budget and Economic Outlook: Fiscal Years 2008 to 2017," available at http://www.cbo.gov.

-- 2007b. "Statement of Robert A. Sunshine: Estimated Costs of US Operations in Iraq and Afghanistan and of Other Activities Related to the War on Terrorism."

-- 2007c. "Statement of Peter Orszag: Estimated Costs of US Operations in Iraq and Afghanistan and of Other Activities Related to the War on Terrorism."

-- 2007d. "Statement of Matthew S. Goldberg: Projecting the Costs to Care for Veterans U.S. Military Operations in Iraq and Afghanistan."

-- 2007e. "Estimated Cost of the Administration's Proposal to Increase the Army's and the Marine Corps's Personnel Levels."

-- 2007f. "Replacing and Repairing Equipment Used in Iraq and Afghanistan: The Army's Reset Program."

-- 2006. "The Economic Effects of Recent Increases in Energy Prices."

Council of Economic Advisors, 2003. "Economic Report of the President." United States Government Printing Office: pp. 54-55.

Day, Jennifer Cheesman and Eric C. Newburger, 2002. "The Big Payoff: Educational Attainment and Synthetic Estimates of Work-Life Earnings." Current Population Reports, United States Census Bureau.

Department of Defense (DOD), 2007. Casualty estimates available at http://www.defenselink.mil/news/casualty.pdf

Energy Information Administration, 2007a. "Cushing, OK West Texas Intermediate (WTI) Spot Price." Available at http://tonto.eia.doe.gov/dnav/pet/hist/rwtcw.htm.

-- 2007b. "World Crude Oil Production, 1960-2006." Available at http://www.eia.doe.gov/emeu/aer/txt/ptb1105.html.

-- 2007c. "Iraq Energy Data, Statistics and Analysis." Available at http://www.eia.doe.gov/cabs/Iraq/Oil.html.

-- 2004. "Energy Security: Oil." Available at http://www.eia.doe.gov/emeu/security/Oil/rule.html.

Friedman, Benjamin M, 2005. "Deficits and Debt in the Short and Long Run." Working paper, National Bureau of Economic Research.

Gomme, Paul, B. Ravikumar, and Peter Rupert, 2006. "The Return of Capital and the Business Cycle." Working Paper, Federal Reserve Bank of Cleveland.

Government Accountability Office, 2006. "Strategic Petroleum Reserve: Available Oil Can Provide Significant Benefits, but Many Factors Should Influence Future Decisions about Fill, Use, and Expansion."

Hamilton, James, 2004. "Oil Shocks and Aggregate Macroeconomic Behavior: The Role of Monetary Policy." *Journal of Money, Credit, and Banking*, 36: 265-286.

Hoge et al, 2004. "Combat Duty in Iraq and Afghanistan, Mental Health Problems, and Barriers to Care." *The New England Journal of Medicine*, 351(1): 13-23.

Huntington, Hillard G, 2005. "The Economic Consequences of Higher Crude Oil Prices." Stanford Energy Modeling Forum report for the US Department of Energy.

Jones, Donald W., Paul N. Leiby, and Inja K. Paik, 2004. "Oil Price Shocks and the Macroeconomy: What Has Been Learned Since 1996." *The Energy Journal*, 25(2).

Kane, Tim, 2004. "Global U.S. Troop Deployment, 1950-2003." The Heritage Foundation.

Kohyama, Hiroyuki, 2006. "Select Discount Rates for Budgetary Purposes." Briefing Paper No. 29, Harvard Law School.

Lyon, Randolph M, 1990. "Federal discount rate policy, the shadow price of capital, and challenges for reforms." *Journal of Environmental Economics and Management*, 18(2.2): S29-S50.

Nordhaus, William, 2007. "Who's Afraid of a Big Bad Oil Shock." Prepared for Brookings Institution Panel on Economic Activity.

Office of Management and Budget (OMB), 1992. "Guidelines and Discount Rates for Benefit-Cost Analysis of Federal Programs." Available at http://www.whitehouse.gov/omb/circulars/a094/a094.html

President's Commission on Care for America's Returning Wounded Warriors (PCCWW), 2007. "Serve, Support, Simplify Report of the President's Commission on Care for America's Returning Wounded Warriors." Available online at http://www.pccww.gov.

Savoca, Elizabeth and Robert Rosenheck, 2000. "The Civilian Labor Market Experiences of Vietnam-Era Veterans: The Influence of Psychiatric Disorders." *The Journal of Mental Health Policy and Economics*, 3: 199-207.

Veterans' Disability Benefits Commission (Veteran's Commission), 2007. Available at http://www.vetscommission.org/.

www.ingramcontent.com/pod-product-compliance
Lightning Source LLC
Chambersburg PA
CBHW080809290526
45790CB00008B/3629